EASY PIANO

MY FIRST JAZZ STANDARDS SONG BOOK

A TREASURY OF FAVORITE SONGS TO PLAY

T0077034

CONTENTS

ISBN 978-1-4950-6289-6

HAL•LEONARD®
CORPORATION
7777 W. BLUEMOUND RD. P.O. BOX 13819 MILWAUKEE, WI 53213

Visit Hal Leonard Online at
www.halleonard.com

WHAT IS A STANDARD?

In music, the term "standard" refers to a popular or jazz composition that has been highly regarded through the years and commonly used as the basis for new arrangements and improvisations. Standards become part of the permanent repertoire of popular song, and are frequently and continually performed throughout the decades by artists of the time. Many standards were originally Tin Pan Alley songs, Broadway show tunes, or songs from Hollywood musicals, and have now become part of the Great American Songbook. Tunes written more recently are well on the way to becoming standards as new interpretations are added by today's popular performers.

Basin Street Blues

Words and Music by
SPENCER WILLIAMS

come a - long with me
to the Mis - sis - sip - pi?

We'll take the boat ___ to the land of dreams, ___

steam down the riv - er down to New Or - leans. ___ The band's there to meet us,

old friends to greet us,

where all the light and the dark folks meet. ___ This is

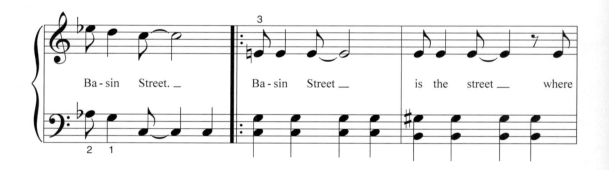

Ba - sin Street. ___ Ba - sin Street ___ is the street ___ where

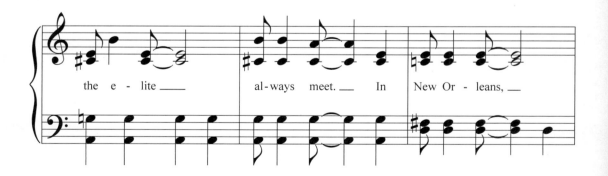

the e - lite ___ al - ways meet. ___ In New Or - leans, ___

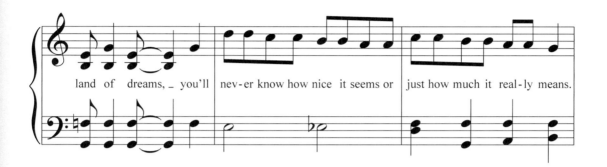

land of dreams, _ you'll nev-er know how nice it seems or just how much it real-ly means.

Glad to be, _____ yes sir - ee, _____ where wel-come's free, _____

dear to me, _____ where I can lose _____ my Ba - sin Street

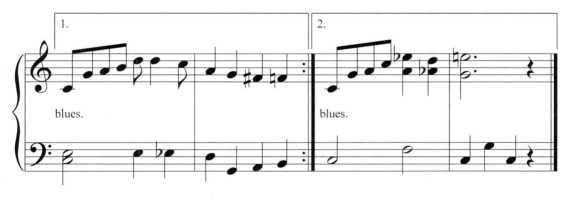

1.
blues.

2.
blues.

Honeysuckle Rose

Words by ANDY RAZAF
Music by THOMAS "FATS" WALLER

With an easy Swing

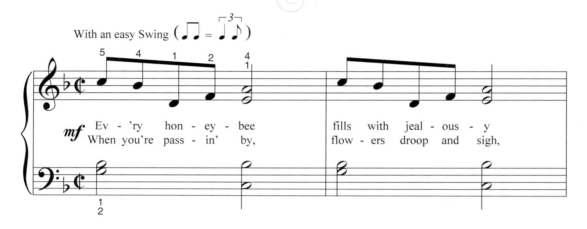

Ev - 'ry hon - ey - bee   fills with jeal - ous - y
When you're pass - in' by,   flow - ers droop and sigh,

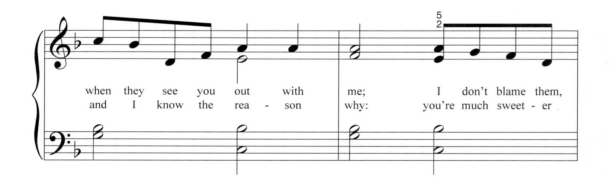

when they see you out with   me;   I don't blame them,
and I know the rea - son   why: you're much sweet - er

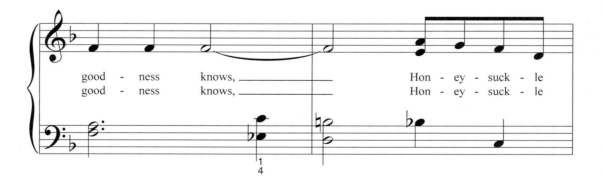

good - ness knows, _____   Hon - ey - suck - le
good - ness knows, _____   Hon - ey - suck - le

Rose. _____

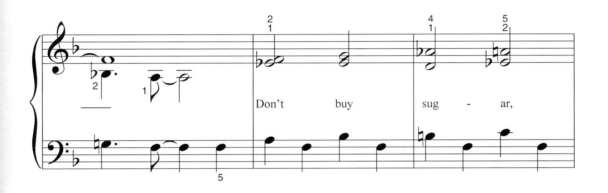

Don't   buy   sug - ar,

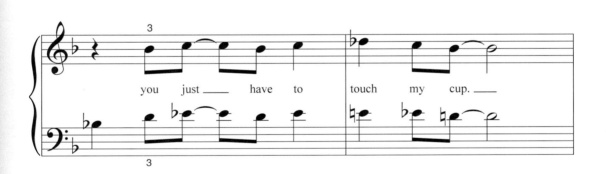

you just ___ have to   touch   my cup. ___

You're   my   sug - ar,   it's sweet _ when you

stir it up. ____ When I'm tak - in' sips from your tas - ty lips

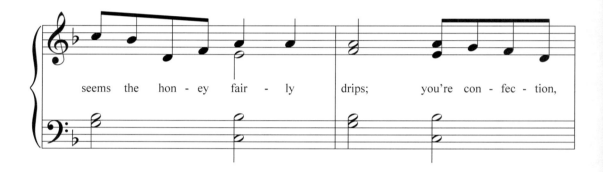

seems the hon - ey fair - ly drips; you're con - fec - tion,

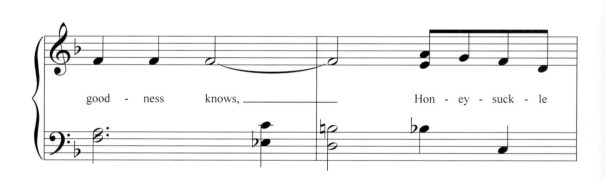

good - ness knows, ____ Hon - ey - suck - le

Rose.

Bye Bye Blackbird

Lyric by MORT DIXON
Music by RAY HENDERSON

Moderately

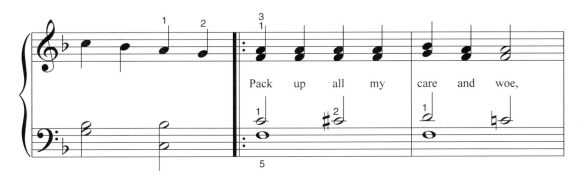

Pack up all my care and woe, here I go sing - ing low; bye

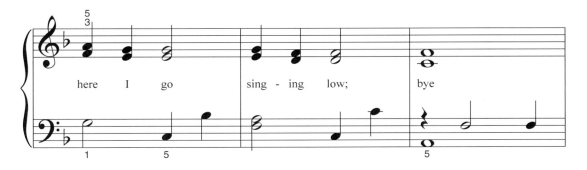

bye black - bird.

Where some - bod - y waits for me, sug - ar's sweet,

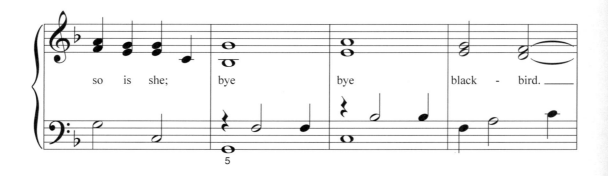

so is she; bye bye black - bird. _____

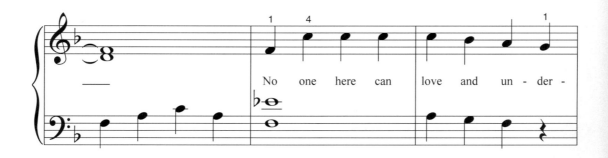

_____ No one here can love and un - der -

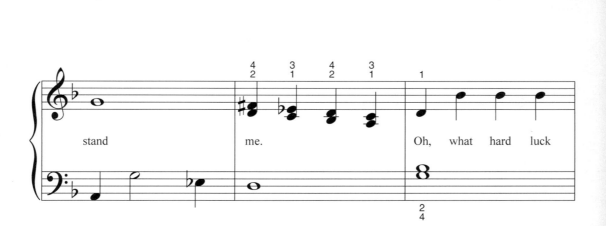

stand me. Oh, what hard luck

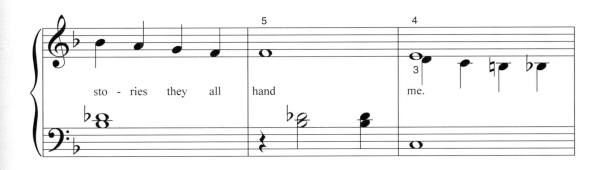

sto - ries they all hand me.

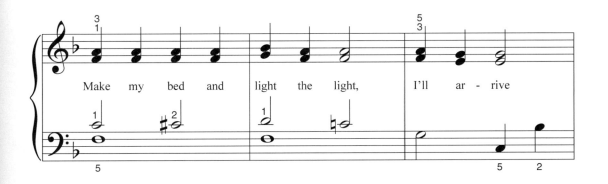

Make my bed and light the light, I'll ar - rive

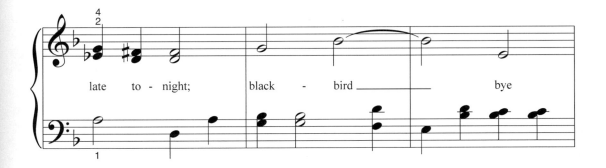

late to - night; black - bird bye

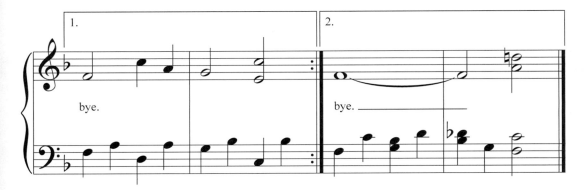

1.

bye.

2.

bye.

SOFTLY AS IN A MORNING SUNRISE

Lyrics by
Oscar Hammerstein II

Music by
Sigmund Romberg

Photo by Hulton Archive/Getty Images

SOFTLY AS IN A MORNING SUNRISE

Lyrics by OSCAR HAMMERSTEIN II
Music by SIGMUND ROMBERG

Tango

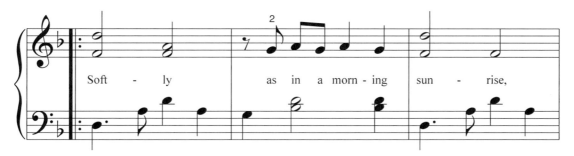

Soft - ly as in a morn - ing sun - rise,

the light of love comes steal - ing in - to a new - born

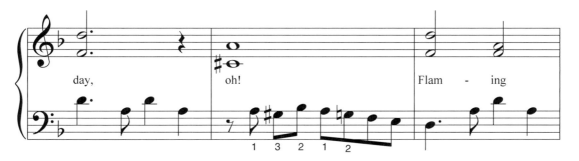

day, oh! Flam - ing

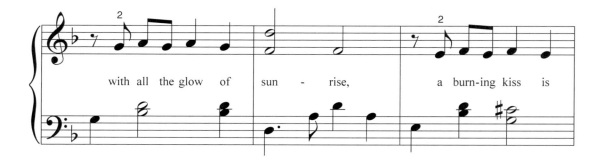

with all the glow of sun - rise, a burn-ing kiss is

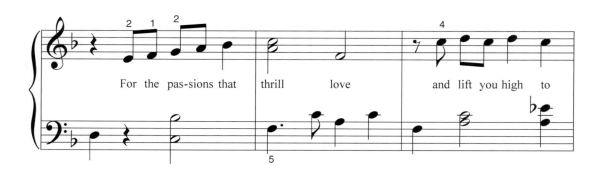

seal - ing the vow that all be - tray.

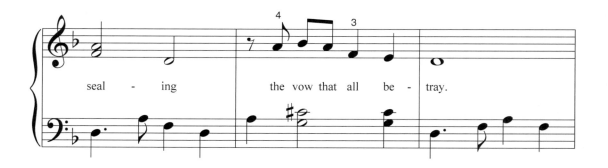

For the pas-sions that thrill love and lift you high to

heav - en are the pas-sions that kill love

and let you fall to hell! So ends each sto - ry.

Soft - ly as in an eve - ning sun - set,

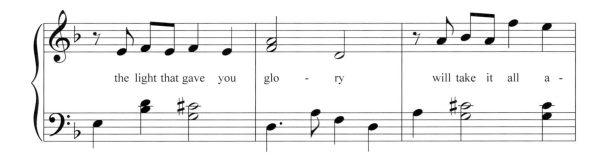

the light that gave you glo - ry will take it all a -

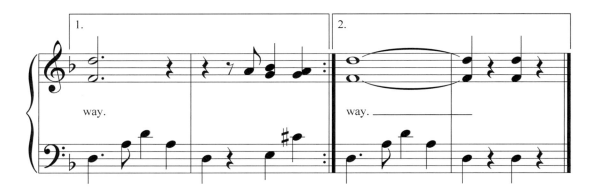

1. way.

2. way.

All the Things You Are

Lyrics by OSCAR HAMMERSTEIN II
Music by JEROME KERN

Slowly, expressively

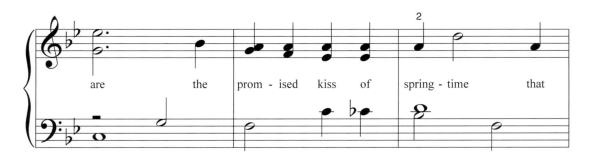

makes the lone - ly win - ter seem long. _____

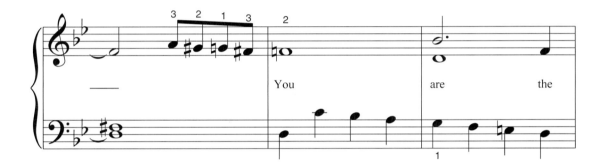

_____ You are the

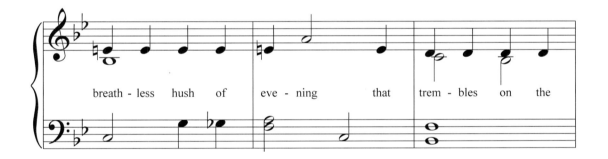

breath - less hush of eve - ning that trem - bles on the

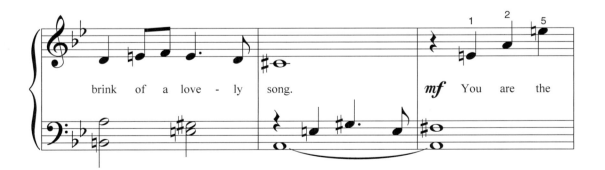

brink of a love - ly song. *mf* You are the

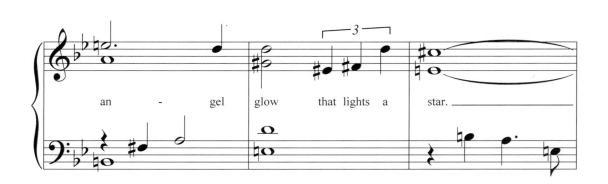

an - gel glow that lights a star. _____

_____ The dear - est things I know are what you

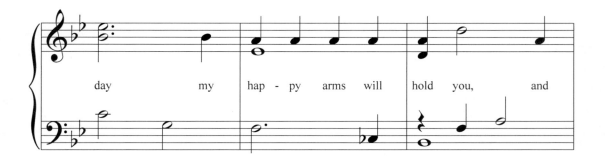

are. Some -

day my hap - py arms will hold you, and

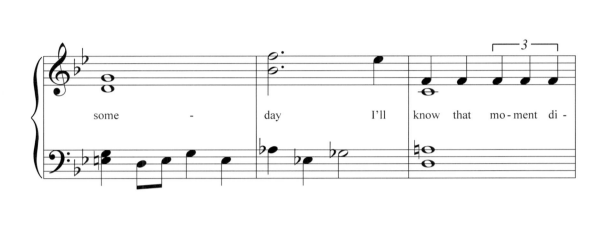

some - day   I'll   know that mo - ment di -

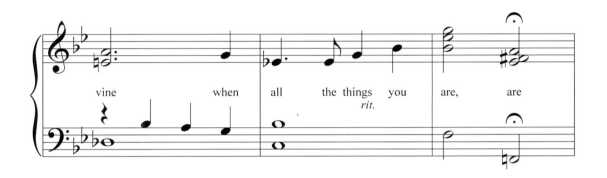

vine   when   all   the things   you   are,   are
rit.

mine.   ***p***
a tempo

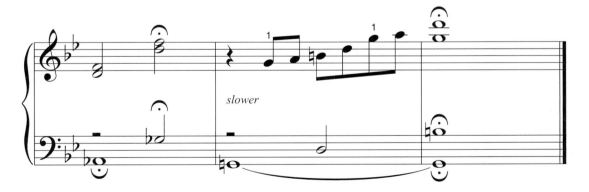

slower

MY FUNNY VALENTINE

Lyrics by
Lorenz Hart

Music by
Richard Rodgers

MY FUNNY VALENTINE

Words by LORENZ HART
Music by RICHARD RODGERS

My fun - ny Val - en - tine, sweet com - ic

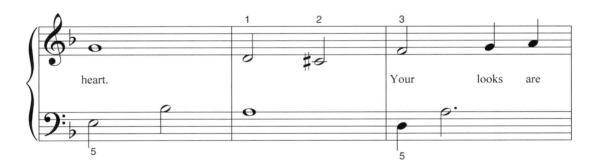

Val - en - tine, you make me smile with my

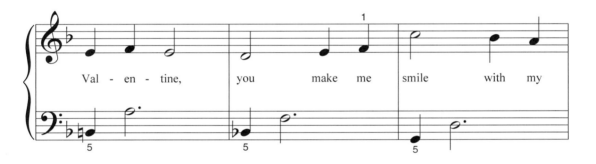

heart. Your looks are

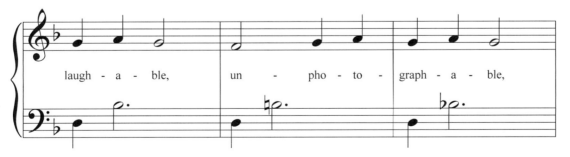

laugh - a - ble, un - pho - to - graph - a - ble,

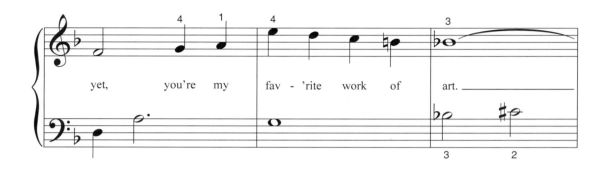

yet,   you're my   fav - 'rite   work   of   art. _____

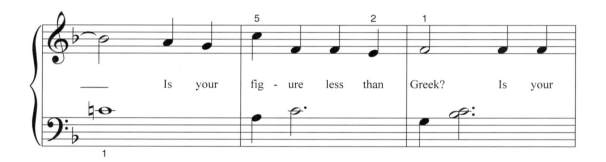

_____   Is   your   fig - ure less than Greek?   Is   your

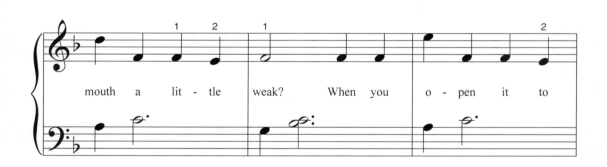

mouth   a   lit - tle   weak?   When you   o - pen it   to

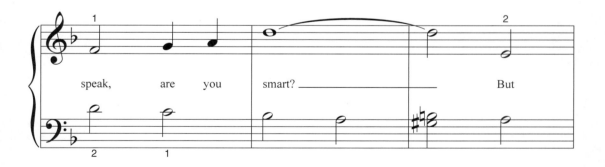

speak,   are you   smart? _____   But

don't   change   a   hair   for   me,   not   if   you

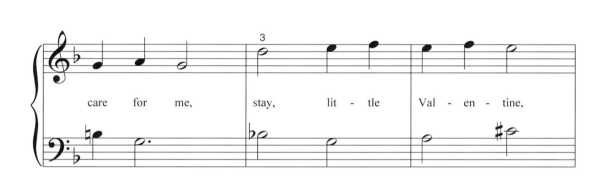

care   for   me,   stay,   lit - tle   Val - en - tine,

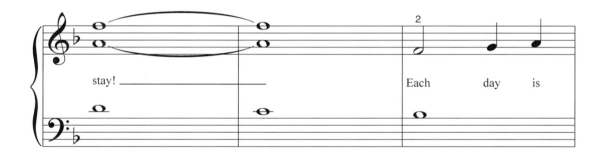

stay! _____   Each   day   is

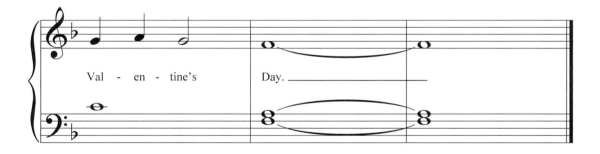

Val - en - tine's   Day. _____

Night and Day

Words and Music by
COLE PORTER

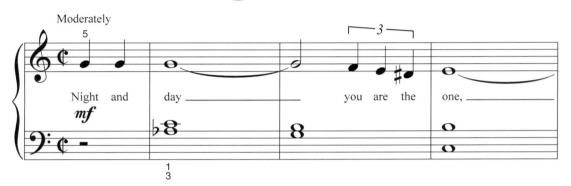

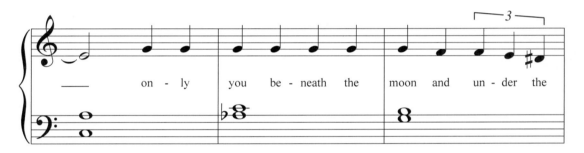

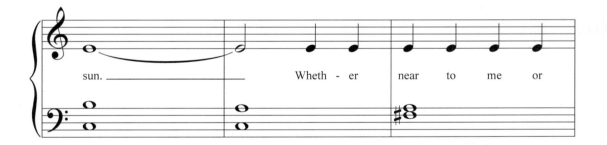

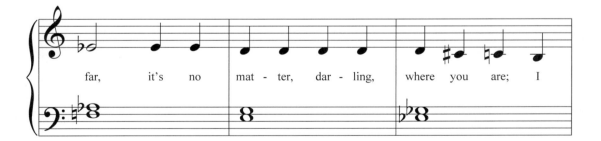

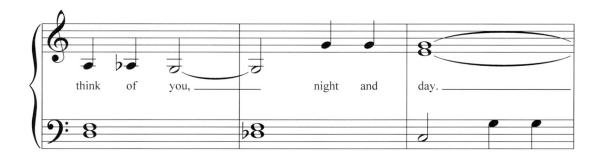

think   of   you, _____   night   and   day. _____

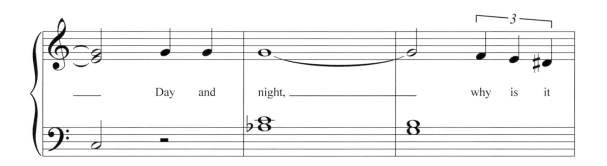

_____ Day   and   night, _____   why   is   it

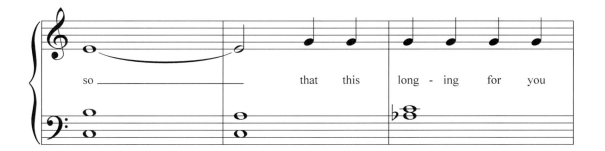

so _____   that   this   long - ing   for   you

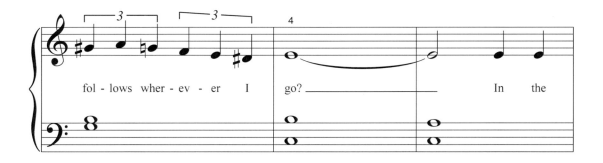

fol - lows wher - ev - er   I   go? _____   In   the

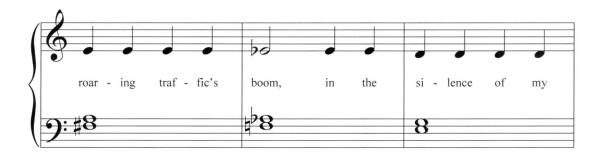

roar - ing traf - fic's boom, in the si - lence of my

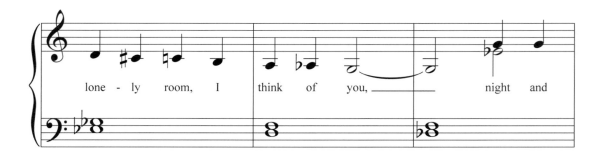

lone - ly room, I think of you, _____ night and

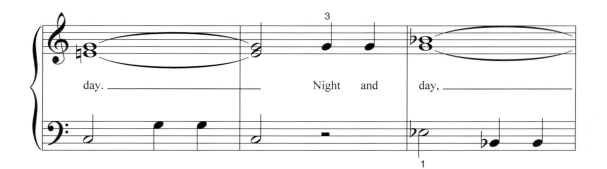

day. _____ Night and day, _____

_____ un - der the hide of me _____ there's an,

oh, such a hun - gry yearn - ing burn - ing in - side of me. _____

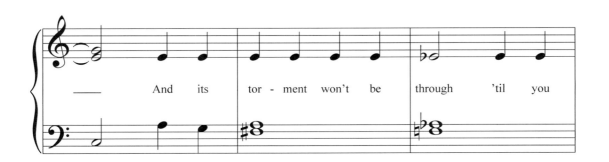

_____ And its tor - ment won't be through 'til you

let me spend my life mak - ing love to you day and night, _____

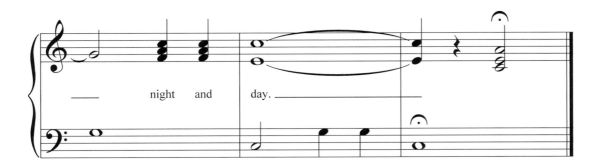

_____ night and day. _____

In a Sentimental Mood

MUSIC BY
DUKE ELLINGTON

Photo courtesy Photofest

In a Sentimental Mood

Words and Music by DUKE ELLINGTON,
IRVING MILLS and MANNY KURTZ

Slowly

In a sen - ti - men - tal

mood, _____ I can see the stars come through my room, ____

kiss _____ drifts a mel - o - dy so strange and sweet ____

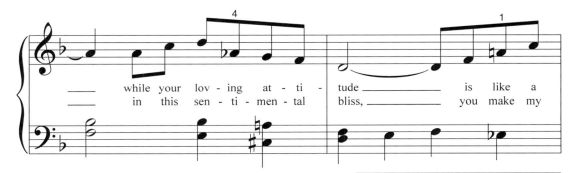

____ while your lov - ing at - ti - tude _____ is like a

____ in this sen - ti - men - tal bliss, _____ you make my

1.

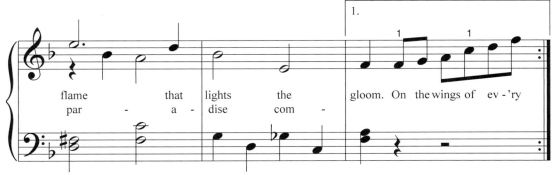

flame   that lights   the   gloom. On the wings of ev - 'ry

par - a - dise   the   com -

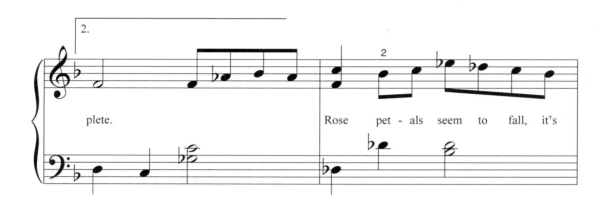

plete.   Rose   pet - als   seem   to   fall,   it's

all   like   a   dream   to   call   you   mine. _____

My   heart's   a   light - er   thing   since

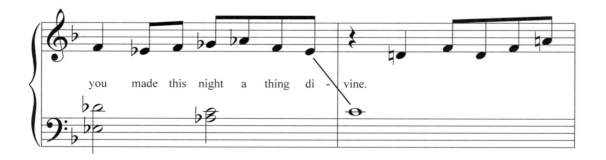

you   made   this   night   a   thing   di -   vine.

In a sen - ti - men - tal mood, _____ I'm with-in a world so

heav - en - ly, _____ for I nev - er dreamt that you'd _____ be lov - ing

To Coda ⊕   **D.S. al Coda (with repeat)**

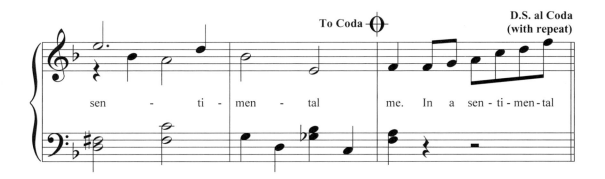

sen - ti - men - tal me. In a sen - ti - men - tal

CODA ⊕

me. *rit.*

Autumn Leaves

English lyric by JOHNNY MERCER
French lyric by JACQUES PREVERT
Music by JOSEPH KOSMA

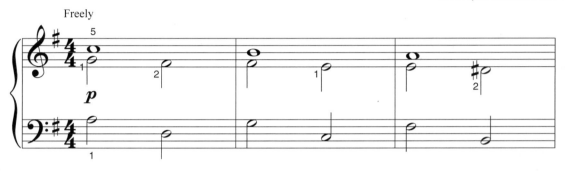

The fall-ing leaves _____ drift by the win-dow, _____ the au-tumn

leaves _____ of red and gold. I see your

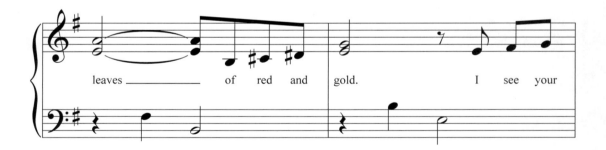

lips, _____ the sum-mer kiss - es, _____ the sun-burned

hands _____ I used to hold. Since you went a - way, __ the days grow

long, _____ and soon I'll hear _____ old win-ter's song. But I

poco rit. *a tempo*

miss you most of all, my dar - ling, when au - tumn leaves start to

fall.

BILLIE'S BOUNCE
(BILL'S BOUNCE)

MUSIC BY
CHARLIE PARKER

BILLIE'S BOUNCE
(BILL'S BOUNCE)

By CHARLIE PARKER

Medium Swing

There Will Never Be Another You

Lyric by MACK GORDON
Music by HARRY WARREN

Moderately

There will be man-y oth-er nights like this, and

_mf_

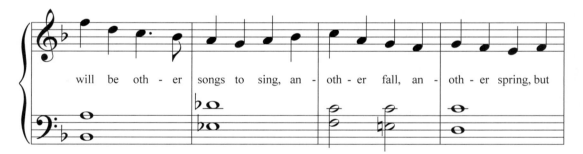

I'll be stand-ing here with some-one new. _____ There

will be oth-er songs to sing, an-oth-er fall, an-oth-er spring, but

there will nev-er be an-oth-er you. There

will   be   oth - er   lips   that   I   may   kiss,   but

they won't thrill me like yours used to   do. _____   Yes,   I may dream a

mil - lion dreams, but how can they come   true,   if   there will nev - er

ev - er   be   an - oth - er   you?

Well You Needn't
(It's Over Now)

Words by MIKE FERRO
Music by THELONIOUS MONK

Fast Swing

LULLABY OF BIRDLAND

Words by GEORGE DAVID WEISS
Music by GEORGE SHEARING

Moderate Swing

Lul - la - by of Bird - land,

that's what I ___ al - ways hear ___ when you sigh. ___

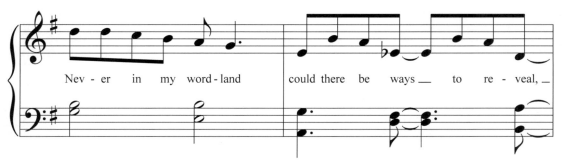

Nev - er in my word - land could there be ways ___ to re - veal, ___

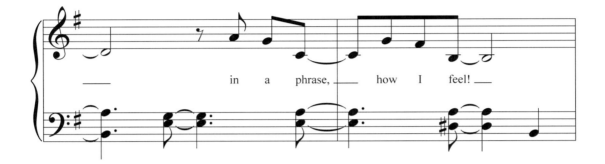

_____ in a phrase, _____ how I feel! _____

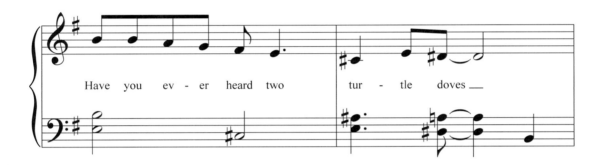

Have you ev - er heard two tur - tle doves _____

bill and coo _____ when they love? _____ That's the kind of mag - ic

mu - sic we make _____ with our lips _____ when we kiss!

And there's a weep-ing old wil-

-low, _____ he real-ly knows how to cry. _

_____ That's how I'd cry on my pil-

-low, _____ if you should tell me fare-well _

Misty

Words by
Johnny Burke

Photo courtesy Photofest

Music by
Erroll Garner

Misty

Words by JOHNNY BURKE
Music by ERROLL GARNER

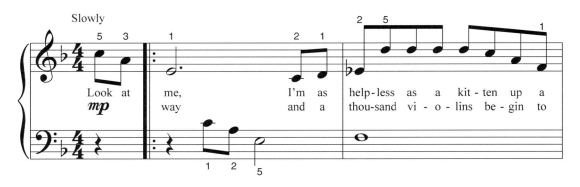

Look at me, I'm as help-less as a kit-ten up a
way and a thou-sand vi-o-lins be-gin to

tree, and I feel like I'm cling-ing to a cloud. I
play, or it might be the sound of your hel-lo, that

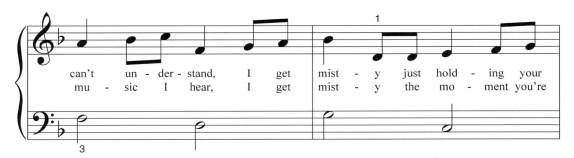

can't un-der-stand, I get mist-y just hold-ing your
mu-sic I hear, I get mist-y the mo-ment you're

hand. Walk my near. _____

You can say that you're lead - ing me on, _____

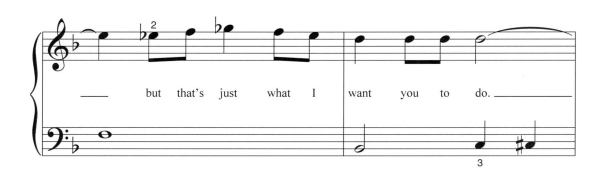

but that's just what I want you to do. _____

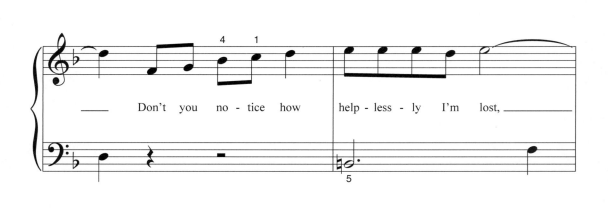

Don't you no - tice how help - less - ly I'm lost, _____

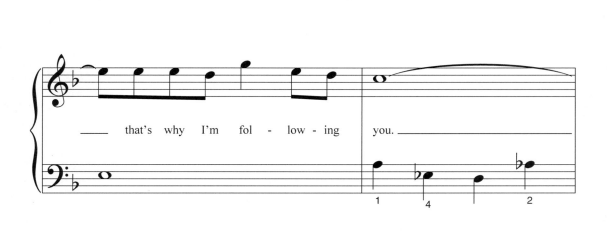

that's why I'm fol - low - ing you. _____

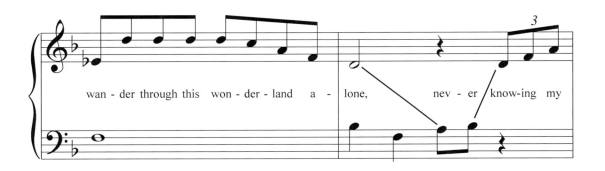

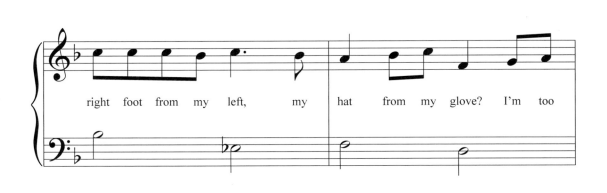

NIGHT TRAIN

Words by OSCAR WASHINGTON
and LEWIS C. SIMPKINS
Music by JIMMY FORREST

Medium Swing

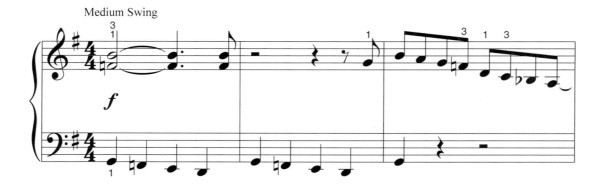

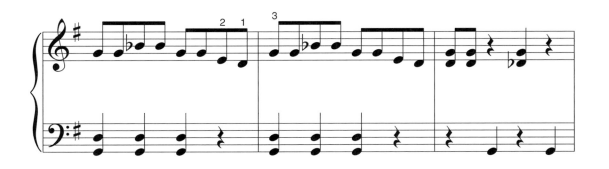

To Coda ⊕

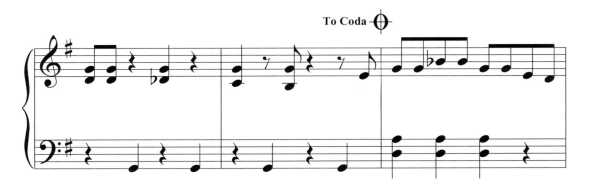

D.C. al Coda

CODA

Words by JOHNNY MERCER
and BILLY STRAYHORN
Music by DUKE ELLINGTON

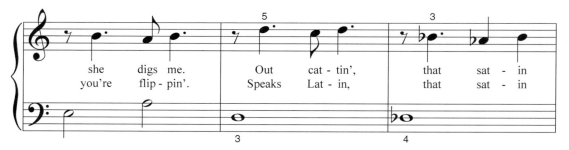

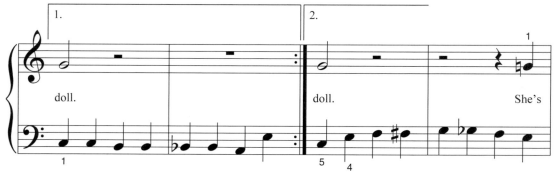

I'll give it a whirl, but I ain't for no girl catch-ing

me. Switch-e - roo · ney. Tel - e - phone num-bers,

well, you know. Do - ing my rhum-bas, with u - no,

and that 'n' my sat - in doll.

SO WHAT

MUSIC BY MILES DAVIS

SO WHAT

By MILES DAVIS

Medium Swing

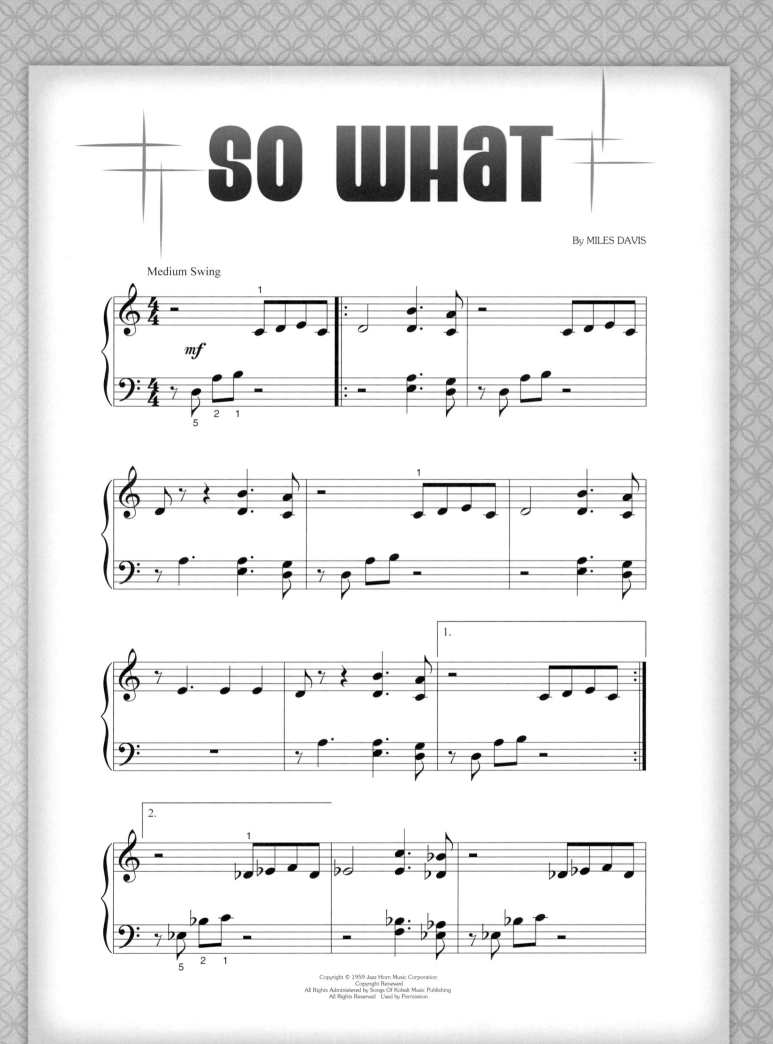

rit.

STOLEN MOMENTS

Words and Music by
OLIVER NELSON

With feeling, not too fast

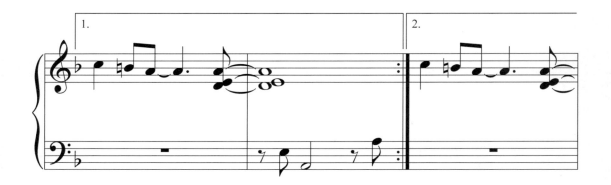

TAKE FIVE

By PAUL DESMOND

Moderately

To Coda

D.S. al Coda

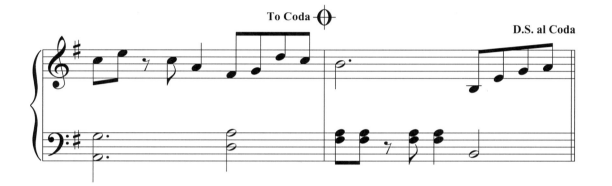

CODA

Bluesette

Words by NORMAN GIMBEL
Music by JEAN THIELEMANS

Moderate Waltz

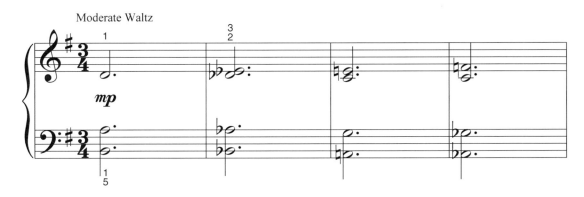

Poor lit - tle sad lit - tle blue Blues - ette,
Long as there's love in your blue heart to share,

don't you cry,
dear Blues - ette,

don't you fret.
don't you des - pair.

You can bet one luck - y day you'll wak - en
Some blue boy is long - ing just like you to

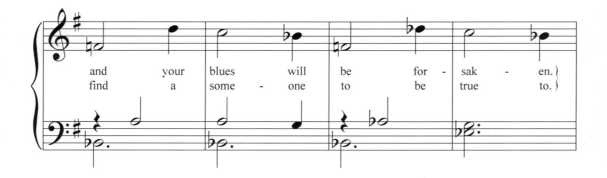

and your blues will be for - sak - en.
find a some - one to be true to.

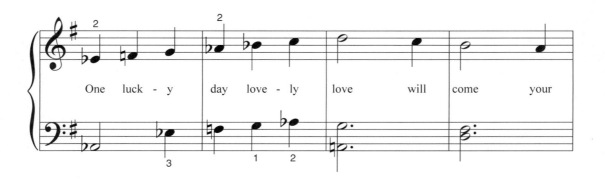

One luck - y day love - ly love will come your

way.

way.

That mag - ic day

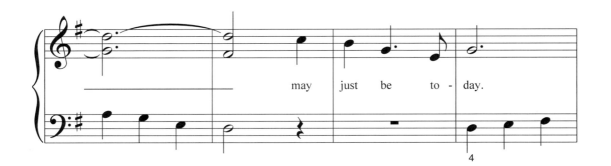

may just be to - day.

BIRDLAND

Words by JON HENDRICKS
Music by JOSEF ZAWINUL

Moderately fast

Five thou-sand light years from the Bird-
Years from the land of the Bird __

- land, but I'm still preach-in' the rhy-
__ and I am still feel-in' the spir-

- thm. _____
- it. _____

Long gone up-tight years from Bird-
Five thou-sand light years from Bird-

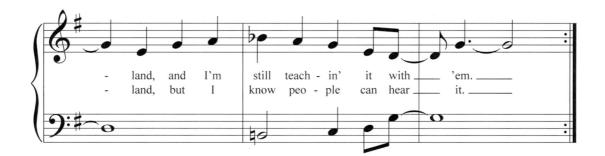

- land, and I'm still teach - in' it with _____ 'em.
- land, but I know peo - ple can hear _____ it. _____

Bird named it, Bird made it, Bird heard it,

then played it. Well stat - ed! _____ Bird - land, _____

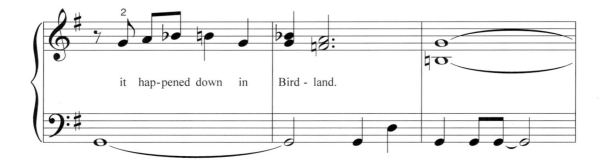

it hap-pened down in Bird - land.

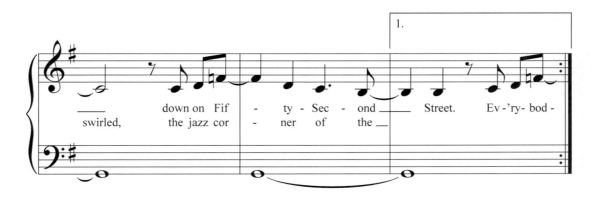

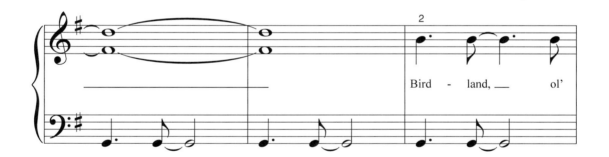

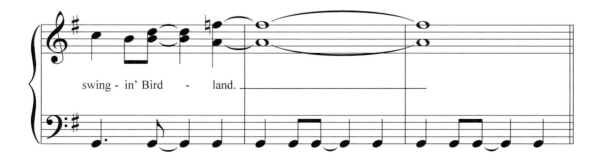

Down them stairs, lose ____ them cares. Where? ____
Bird would cook, Max ____ would look. Where? ____

Down in Bird - land. To - tal swing, bop ____
Down in Bird - land. Miles came through, 'Trane ____

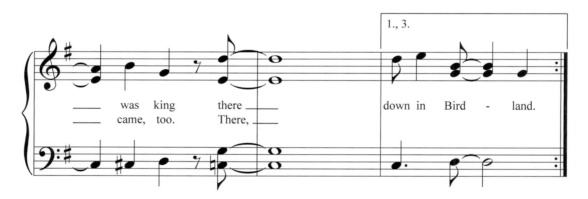

____ was king there ____ | down in Bird - land.
____ came, too. There, ____ |

down in Bird - land. | Ba - sie blew, Blak -

-ey, too.   Where? ___   Down in Bird - land.

To Coda ⊕

Can - non - ball   played ___   that   hall.   There, ___

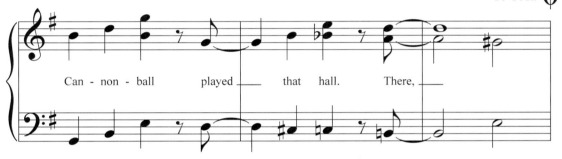

down in   Bird - land.

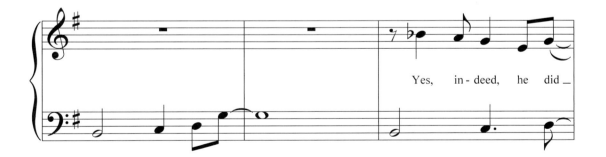

Yes,   in - deed,   he   did ___

Yard - bird Par - ker played in Bird -

- land. _____ Yes, in - deed, he real - ly did, _____

D.S. al Coda
(with repeat)

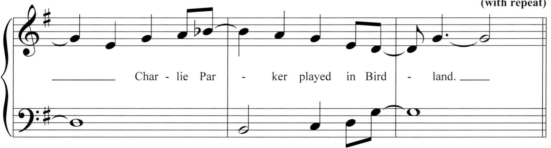

_____ Char - lie Par - ker played in Bird - land. _____

CODA

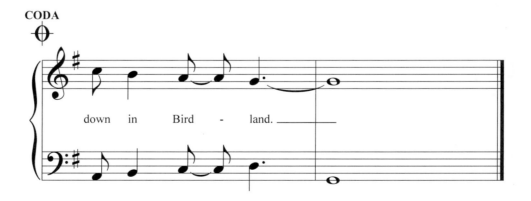

down in Bird - land. _____

SPAIN

By CHICK COREA

Freely, rubato

Bright Latin Tempo

To Coda ⊕

D.S. al Coda

CODA

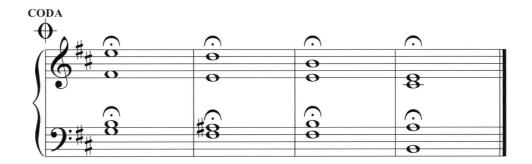

Little Sunflower

Music by
Freddie Hubbard

Little Sunflower

By FREDDIE HUBBARD

Medium Latin

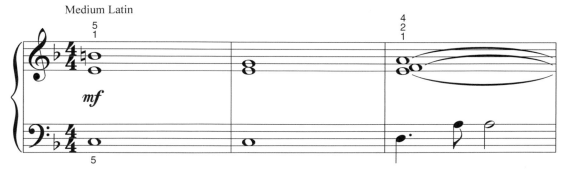

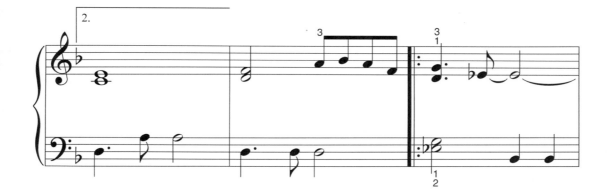

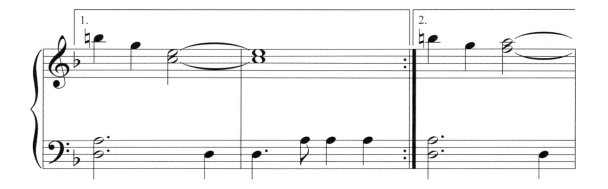

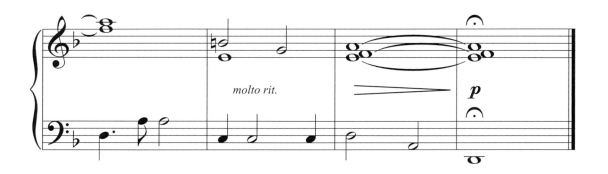

molto rit.

p

WATERMELON MAN

By HERBIE HANCOCK

Medium Rock

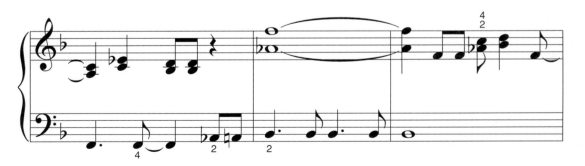

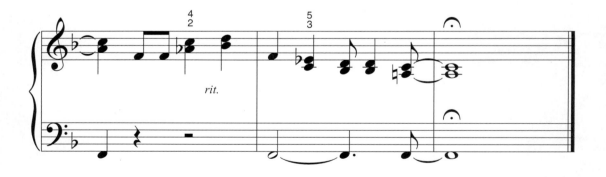